Samuel French Acting Edition

Hamlet II
(Better than the Original)

A New Comedy by
Sam Bobrick

Original Story by
William Shakespeare

SAMUELFRENCH.COM   SAMUELFRENCH.CO.UK

Copyright © 1983, 1985 by Sam Bobrick
All Rights Reserved

HAMLET II is fully protected under the copyright laws of the United States of America, the British Commonwealth, including Canada, and all other countries of the Copyright Union. All rights, including professional and amateur stage productions, recitation, lecturing, public reading, motion picture, radio broadcasting, television and the rights of translation into foreign languages are strictly reserved.

ISBN 978-0-573-61983-0

www.SamuelFrench.com
www.SamuelFrench.co.uk

FOR PRODUCTION ENQUIRIES

UNITED STATES AND CANADA
Info@SamuelFrench.com
1-866-598-8449

UNITED KINGDOM AND EUROPE
Plays@SamuelFrench.co.uk
020-7255-4302

Each title is subject to availability from Samuel French, depending upon country of performance. Please be aware that *HAMLET II* may not be licensed by Samuel French in your territory. Professional and amateur producers should contact the nearest Samuel French office or licensing partner to verify availability.

CAUTION: Professional and amateur producers are hereby warned that *HAMLET II* is subject to a licensing fee. Publication of this play(s) does not imply availability for performance. Both amateurs and professionals considering a production are strongly advised to apply to Samuel French before starting rehearsals, advertising, or booking a theatre. A licensing fee must be paid whether the title(s) is presented for charity or gain and whether or not admission is charged. Professional/Stock licensing fees are quoted upon application to Samuel French.

No one shall make any changes in this title(s) for the purpose of production. No part of this book may be reproduced, stored in a retrieval system, or transmitted in any form, by any means, now known or yet to be invented, including mechanical, electronic, photocopying, recording, videotaping, or otherwise, without the prior written permission of the publisher. No one shall upload this title(s), or part of this title(s), to any social media websites.

For all enquiries regarding motion picture, television, and other media rights, please contact Samuel French.

MUSIC USE NOTE

Licensees are solely responsible for obtaining formal written permission from copyright owners to use copyrighted music in the performance of this play and are strongly cautioned to do so. If no such permission is obtained by the licensee, then the licensee must use only original music that the licensee owns and controls. Licensees are solely responsible and liable for all music clearances and shall indemnify the copyright owners of the play(s) and their licensing agent, Samuel French, against any costs, expenses, losses and liabilities arising from the use of music by licensees. Please contact the appropriate music licensing authority in your territory for the rights to any incidental music.

IMPORTANT BILLING AND CREDIT REQUIREMENTS

If you have obtained performance rights to this title, please refer to your licensing agreement for important billing and credit requirements.

CHARACTERS

*(By doubling certain parts,
only seven to nine actors are necessary.)*

HAMLET .... Prince of Denmark

GERTRUDE ... Queen of Denmark, Hamlet's mother

CLAUDIUS .... King of Denmark, Hamlet's uncle

GHOST .... Ghost of Denmark, Hamlet's father

HORATIO..................... Hamlet's best friend

POLONIUS..................... Lord Chamberlain

LAERTES......................... Son to Polonius

OPHELIA..................... Daughter to Polonius

ROSENCRANTZ .... A college friend of Hamlet's

GUILDENSTERN .... Ditto

FRANCISCO............................ A soldier

BERNARDO .... Another soldier

GRAVEDIGGER..................... A gravedigger

HAMLET II
(BETTER THAN THE ORIGINAL)

ACT I
SCENE 1

The setting is the royal castle in Elsinore. The year is 1217. The night air is cold and foggy. FRANCISCO, a chilled and anxious soldier, stands guard on a platform before the castle. In the distance the tower clock strikes twelve. HORATIO, Hamlet's best friend, approaches cautiously.

FRANCISCO. Who's there?

HORATIO. Me, Horatio. Did it appear yet, Francisco?

FRANCISCO. No. But soon, I'm sure.

HORATIO. I don't know why I let you drag me up here. It's Saturday night, wenching and whoring time.

FRANCISCO. True, Horatio, but how often does one get to see a ghost? If it's like the other nights, it should be here any minute.

HORATIO. A ghost on our shores. This forebodes ill times for Denmark.

FRANCISCO. You always say that, Horatio.

HORATIO. I only said it twice. Once now and once when the sardines went bad. Ssssshh! I think I see something.

FRANCISCO. It's the ghost!

(The GHOST of the late king appears in a white sheet.)

GHOST. Ooooooooooooooooo!
HORATIO. Oh, my God!
FRANCISCO. Does it not look like the old dead King himself?
GHOST. Ooooooooooooooooo!
FRANCISCO. Go, Horatio. Speak to it. You went to college.
HORATIO. *(to GHOST)* Welcome to Denmark. Would you like to buy some stark but practical furniture? *(The GHOST looks at them and walks off.)* Well, one thing is certain. He's not here to shop.
FRANCISCO. I swear, it's the ghost of the old dead King. It looks just like him.
HORATIO. All dead kings look alike. It could also be the dead Queen of Poland.
FRANCISCO. Not so. The dead Queen of Poland still lives. Mark these words. There's always trouble when a dead king's ghost shows up.

(The GHOST returns.)

HORATIO. It's coming back.
FRANCISCO. Should I give it a taste of my sword?
HORATIO. No. You might kill it. *(to GHOST)* What is it, Ghost? Who are you? You look weary, troubled. Speak, you pathetic apparition! *(The GHOST turns around, drops his pants and moons at them. They look on in horror.)*

FRANCISCO. He doth moon! Oh, my God. That wart on his ass. The shape of a gherkin. It *is* the old King. *(The GHOST exits.)*

HORATIO. Francisco, I have a feeling what we are here witnessing is only the beginning of a great story that might very well make Denmark almost as sad and dreary a place as anybody's home town.

FRANCISCO. Oh, shucks. *(They start off.)*

BLACKOUT

Scene 2

The throne room of the castle. It is daytime. BERNARDO, KING CLAUDIUS and QUEEN GERTRUDE followed by POLONIUS and OPHELIA enter.

BERNARDO. *(pounding a staff)* All hail the King! *(CLAUDIUS and GERTRUDE walk to the throne.)*

VOICES. *(on and off stage)*
What sayeth thou, King?
How goest thou, King?
How be'est thou, King?
(CLAUDIUS and GERTRUDE sit on their throne — the crowd continues to buzz.)

CLAUDIUS. All right. Let's quiet down. Got a few things to say here.

POLONIUS. *(pounding BERNARDO's staff)* Hark, hark

and all that nonsense! *(The crowd quiets down.)*
CLAUDIUS. Thank you, Polonius.
POLONIUS. My pleasure.
CLAUDIUS. *(to crowd)* Look, first I want to clear the air. Now I know it looks kind of suspicious, my brother, Harold, the late King, just being dead a couple of months and me marrying his widowed wife, the exciting and sensuous Gertrude, and becoming King... *(The crowd ad-libs agreement.)*
CROWD.
Very suspicious!
It's the talk of the town!
Shameful!
Scandalous!...
CLAUDIUS. Okay, let me just say, the next smartass to point that out eats every meal in the castle cafeteria for a year.
CROWD. *(ad-libs)*
What a nice couple!
Aren't they cute!
I'm so happy for them!
CLAUDIUS. I love being King. It's a good job with good hours, and I mean to keep it. I'll do my best to be just and maybe even fair.
CROWD. Just and maybe fair. Isn't that big of him.
CLAUDIUS. *(putting arm around GERTRUDE)* All I can tell you is that me and the little woman, well, we're as happy as two flies in a pile of dung, and for these trying times, that's not half bad.
GERTRUDE. My Claudius has such a way with words.
CLAUDIUS. You bet. Now let's get on with the business

of the day.
POLONIUS. Taxes!
CLAUDIUS. Raise them.
POLONIUS. Living standards.
CLAUDIUS. Lower them.
POLONIUS. Norway.
CLAUDIUS. What about Norway?
POLONIUS. They want to attack us.
CLAUDIUS. For what? We've got crap here. Send a very ugly person to Norway to tell them that.
POLONIUS. *(indicating BERNARDO)* You!
BERNARDO. Thanks a lot!
CLAUDIUS. Next!
POLONIUS. It's my son, Laertes, your Lordship. He'd like permission to attend school in France.
CLAUDIUS. Ahh, that's great. Higher education. I'm for that. I was never able to finish high school because when I was a kid, we were very poor rich people. But for a youth today to want to pursue reading and writing and all that poppycock, I take my crown off to him. What is it young Laertes aspires to be?
POLONIUS. *(proudly)* I'll let him tell you himself, my Lord. *(calling into the crowd)* Larry!

(LAERTES steps forward. He is quite the fop.)

POLONIUS. *(Puts his arm around LAERTES proudly.)* Tell him, my son.
LAERTES. *(producing a comb)* A hairdresser, your Highness.
GERTRUDE. *(applauding)* Bravo! Bravo! A hairdresser.

Book me in for a wash, a rinse and a blow dry.

POLONIUS. *(to GERTRUDE)* I was so worried he might go into the arts.

CLAUDIUS. Go to France with our blessing, Laertes, and may you never, in your lifetime, know a bad quiche Lorraine.

LAERTES. Thank you, Your Highness. *(LAERTES exits.)*

BERNARDO. All hail, Prince Hamlet! *(Everyone moans.)*

(HAMLET appears. He is brooding and morose. He has a rose in his hand. He puts it to his nose.)

HAMLET. A rose by any other name would smell as sweet. Yet, if it were called a cankersore, I would not buy one. *(He discards the rose.)*

GERTRUDE. Look at him. He's so sad, so gloomy.

CLAUDIUS. This must be one of his better days.

GERTRUDE. *(Stretches out hands toward HAMLET.)* Come to me, my melancholy baby. Come to me and don't be blue.

HAMLET. *(Walks slowly to his mother and kneels at her side.)* My Lady, my Lord.

GERTRUDE. Nonsense. We're just plain Mom and Dad. Tell him, Claudius.

CLAUDIUS. That's right, young man. Things are going to go on just as usual. Nothing's changed except maybe on Father's Day you won't have much to do.

HAMLET. *(turning back on CLAUDIUS)* Very funny. Ha ha.

GERTRUDE. Dead is dead, Hamlet. I know you miss

your father. Yet know we not why, things sometimes happen for the best. *(She nudges CLAUDIUS playfully.)* If I tell you how long this man can go at night, you won't believe it.

CLAUDIUS. *(proudly)* It's wheat germ. I put wheat germ on everything.

GERTRUDE. Be happy for me, dear Hamlet. I am once again a complete woman ... with good skin.

HAMLET. I am happy for you, dear Mother.

GERTRUDE. Then show it. Come on, give Mumsie a little kiss.

HAMLET. Must I? In front of all these people?

GERTRUDE. He always was a shy little thing.

HAMLET. Very well. As you like it. *(He kisses his mother on the cheek.)*

GERTRUDE. No, no, not on the cheek. That's no kiss. Kiss like we always kiss.

HAMLET. Yes, Mother. *(He takes GERTRUDE in his arms and kisses her passionately on the lips.)*

CLAUDIUS. *(Looks on in alarm.)* No tongue! No tongue! *(HAMLET and GERTRUDE break.)*

GERTRUDE. Now, isn't that better?

HAMLET. I guess so.

GERTRUDE. I pity thee, Claudius. You'll never know what it's like to be a mother.

CLAUDIUS. All right. It's half past eleven. Time to watch the new prisoners get tortured.

GERTRUDE. *(to HAMLET)* Oh, what fun! Will you join us, Hamlet?

HAMLET. No, thanks. I have no wish for merriment.

GERTRUDE. Well, maybe another day.

CLAUDIUS. I can hardly wait. Now off to the dungeons. *(to HAMLET)* So long, sour puss. *(As they exit, HAMLET sticks his tongue out at the King.)*

HAMLET. *(Now left alone.)* Oh, that this too solid flesh would melt. *(a beat)* What the hell does that mean? I miss my dead father. But a lot of thirty-year-old men miss their dead fathers. And my mother, for her to marry such a swine as my Uncle Claudius. And so strict a monarch is he. No longer am I permitted to crawl into bed with them when I have bad dreams. Sometimes I wonder whether it's worth going on. Ahhh, to be or not to be? That is the question.

(HORATIO enters.)

HORATIO. Hail to your Lordship.

HAMLET. *(annoyed)* Damn, I was just getting into myself.

HORATIO. My Majesty, I'm going to lay something heavy on thee. Hopest that thou art prepared to accept it in the bravest of fashion.

HAMLET. Hey, come on. I'm a prince. I'm royalty. I'm made of sterling.

HORATIO. It scared the b-jesus out of me.

HAMLET. I'm nobility. They don't make 'em tougher than this royal Danish.

HORATIO. Okay. Last night on the castle wall I saw the ghost of your dead father.

HAMLET. *(sarcastic)* The ghost of my father. *(He takes a beat and then faints into HORATIO'S arms.)*

BLACKOUT

Scene 3

Laertes' bedroom. Stage right. LAERTES is packing several suitcases. OPHELIA is rolling a joint.

LAERTES. Listen, Sis, I'm not a prude, but when I'm gone, I want you to stop hanging around with Hamlet.
OPHELIA. Oh, come on, Laertes. I'm not a kid anymore. I'm thirteen.
LAERTES. It's all over the palace about you two. How do you think I feel every time I walk into a public bathroom and there painted on the walls is "Ophelia Doth Not Protest Too Much."
OPHELIA. That's just everyday Danish graffiti.
LAERTES. Well, I don't like it. If Hamlet wants to fool around, there are other guy's sisters, but my sister's off limits. My sister saves it till just before she gets married.
OPHELIA. Laertes, when are you going to learn sex doesn't have to be dirty?
LAERTES. Yes, it does.
OPHELIA. No, it doesn't.
LAERTES. Yes, it does or else it's no fun at all.

(POLONIUS enters.)

POLONIUS. Hurry, Laertes, your ride to France is

downstairs. *(sniffing)* What's that smell?
OPHELIA. *(taking another drag)* Nothing.
POLONIUS. Now, Son, I just want to give you a little fatherly advice before you go.
LAERTES. *(sighs)* Do you have to?
POLONIUS. It's expected of me. Okay, here it is, short and sweet. Neither a borrower nor a lender be. But if you have to, borrow at 8%, loan at 15%. And above all, and this could be the most important thing I'll ever tell you. To thine own self be true. Never trust a talking chicken.
LAERTES. How wise thou art.
POLONIUS. Except Sundays. That's my day off.
LAERTES. *(Takes his bags.)* Goodbye, Dad.
POLONIUS. Goodbye, Son.
LAERTES. Goodbye, Ophelia. Remember what I told you about Hamlet. *(He leaves.)*
POLONIUS. What's this about you and Hamlet?
OPHELIA. Nothing.
POLONIUS. What do you mean, nothing? I'm the Lord Chamberlain in this town. I've got a reputation to uphold. Has it got something to do with sex?
OPHELIA. Sex is a very normal thing.
POLONIUS. *(alarmed)* I'm ruined! Okay, what did he do? Did he touch your no-no's? You let him touch your no-no's? Who else knows he touched your no-no's?
OPHELIA. I love the kind and confused Lord Hamlet and nothing you do or say will make me change the way I feel. Now I'm going to my room. *(She exits.)*
POLONIUS. Goddamn Hamlet. If he wasn't the boss' son, I'd kick his butt. How can you do this to a loving

father? *(shouting after OPHELIA)* Someday when you have children of your own, I hope they screw around. Boy oh boy. If it's tough raising kids in the year 1217, what's going to happen in the future when they start living longer?

BLACKOUT

Scene 4

The castle platform. It is night. HAMLET, HORATIO, and FRANCISCO approach.

FRANCISCO. This is where we always see it at just about this time.
HAMLET. The ghost of my dead father.
HORATIO. Aye, my Lord.
HAMLET. All right, guys, cut the crap. You got me up here. What is it? A surprise party? *(shouting)* Come on, everyone, yell "Surprise!" Bring out the cheese dip and Danish ham., You guys did this to cheer me up. I feel better already. The hell with my mother and uncle. I'll get over it. Come on! Out from your hiding places and let's all sing. *(singing)*
HAPPY BIRTHDAY, HAMLET,
YOU'VE LIVED ANOTHER YEAR,
WE NEVER THOUGHT YOU'D MAKE IT.
NOW OPEN UP THE BEER.

(The GHOST appears.)

GHOST. What the hell's the racket? It's night time. People are trying to sleep.

HAMLET. Father!

GHOST. *(He has a cigar.)* Mind if I smoke?

HAMLET. Father!

GHOST. Hi, Son. How's life? *(He lights his cigar.)*

HAMLET. Father! Dear, sweet, noble father. Let me touch you. Let me embrace you.

GHOST. No, thanks. I saw what you do with your mother. Listen, Son, I'm in a bit of a jam and I could use your help.

HAMLET. Whatever you want, Father. Whatever you need.

GHOST. It's kind of personal. *(He indicates HORATIO and FRANCISCO.)*

FRANCISCO. We'll be around the corner if you need us.

HORATIO. You're looking good, old dead King.

GHOST. Thanks, fellas. *(HORATIO and FRANCISCO exit.)* Nice boys, but if you want to be smart, keep them away from Ophelia.

HAMLET. Pray telleth now, dear father, what brings thy ghostly body to these haunts?

GHOST. Well, it's like this. I was under a tree in my pear orchard taking a snooze when your Uncle Claudius came over and poisoned my ear.

HAMLET. He poisoned your ear? Of all the stupid ways to kill someone.

GHOST. Take it from a guy who was there, it works.

HAMLET. So it *was* Uncle Claudius. I knew he had

something to do with it.

GHOST. He wanted my crown and your mother. You know, even when we were kids, he was a twit. He rode my horse, he stole my toys, he kicked my peasant, but he was the youngest child so he got away with it.

HAMLET. Sometimes parents are so unfair.

GHOST. Anyway, I'm dead now and I want to go to heaven, except they got a rule that says, if you're murdered and your son doesn't avenge you, you can't go. So what do you say, Hamlet, do you want to get involved?

HAMLET. You ... want me to kill Uncle Claudius?

GHOST. That's right. Nothing too elaborate. A cut throat, a dagger in the heart, a bad piece of fish...

HAMLET. I ... I don't know. Killing a living human being. What if I just had him beaten up and tossed in the dungeon?

GHOST. No good. Got to kill him. Rules of heaven.

HAMLET. Look, can I have a few days to think it over?

GHOST. No! I know you, Hamlet. Once you start thinking about things, it's forever. You never were terrific about making up your mind.

HAMLET. To be or not to be. That is the question. Whether 'tis nobler to avenge my father and maybe end up in jail for twenty years, or to ignore this whole rotten day and live happily ever after.

GHOST. Avenge me, or I'll tell everyone your real name is Betty.

HAMLET. *(quickly)* I'll avenge you, sweet Father, if it's the last thing I do.

GHOST. It's gotta be the first thing you do. If it's the last thing you do, I'm in trouble.
HAMLET. What about Mother? Do you want me to kill her, too?
GHOST. No, I don't think so. Her punishment will be when she finds out how hard it is for a woman in her forties to start dating again. See you around, Hamlet.
HAMLET. Wait! One other thing, sweet Father.
GHOST. Make it fast. I've only got till the cock crows.
HAMLET. That's okay. Today we turned the cocks back an hour. I want to know. What's it like to be dead?
GHOST. Have you ever been to New Jersey? *(The GHOST exits.)*
HAMLET. *(a beat)* What did'st I see? Did'st I see what I did'st see, or did'st I see what onc't I thought I did'st saw? Nay! Yet yay! But nay! Yet, how can I be sure that was the true ghost of my father or the work of the Devil? I've got to be sure I'm not being tricked. I've got to be sure that Uncle Claudius is the culprit. I've also got to stop talking aloud to myself, or else they're going to lock me up. *(calling)* Horatio! Francisco! Come out, come out, wherever you are. Olly olly oxen free! There is treachery afoot.

(HORATIO and FRANCISCO appear.)

HORATIO. My Lord.
FRANCISCO. Betty!
HAMLET. These are times that try men's souls. I now have the opportunity and choice to be known as Hamlet, the great and tragic Prince of Denmark, or Hamlet, just

another every day asshole. Either one has its merits. Alas, 'tis all words, for my highway is chosen. *(He draws his sword.)* Come hither, gentlemen, and lay your hands upon my sword, never to speak of this that you have heard.

HORATIO. Be you serious, my Lord?

HAMLET. Must I thus, for why would I speak such fine English if I wasn't?

FRANCISCO. That's Danish.

HAMLET. What?

FRANCISCO. It's Danish we're speaking.

HAMLET. I stand corrected. I've been chosen to right the wrongs that have been wronged. I want your promise that all this which we have witnessed shall be spoken nevermore.

HORATIO. I swear.

FRANCISCO. I swear.

HAMLET. And I swear.

HORATIO. You don't have to. Just us.

HAMLET. That's right. Just you.

FRANCISCO. And me.

HAMLET. And me.

HORATIO. *(impatient)* Not you! Us!

HAMLET. Okay, okay. I'm new at this. *(HORATIO and FRANCISCO take their hands off the sword.)* Wait! One more thing. *(The two men put their hands back on the sword.)* If in pursuit of my noble purpose I must pretend madness, you must not give the slightest indication that you are aware of the reason.

FRANCISCO. Madness? For what reason?

HAMLET. I said not thee asketh. Just swear.

HORATIO. I swear, my beloved Prince.
FRANCISCO. I swear, my noble Lord.
HORATIO. I swear, my royal Majesty.
FRANCISCO. I swear, my magnificent monarch.
HAMLET. Good. *(He pulls the sword from their fingertips to put back in his sheath. In doing so, he cuts the fingers of his friends. They jump in pain.)*
FRANCISCO. Big dummy!
HORATIO. Goofy bastard!
FRANCISCO. Crazy maniac!
HAMLET. *(apologetic)* Sorry about that. Hope none of you guys play piano. *(They start off.)*

BLACKOUT

Scene 5

A series of blackouts at the castle. CLAUDIUS and GERTRUDE are fast asleep on their thrones. GERTRUDE is awakened by the crowing of a rooster. She shakes CLAUDIUS.

HAMLET. *(offstage)* Cock-a-doodle-doo! Cock-a-doodle-doo!
GERTRUDE. Claudius. Claudius. The cock doth crow.
CLAUDIUS. *(punchy)* Please, not again.
GERTRUDE. It doth crow.
CLAUDIUS. Doth not.
GERTRUDE. Doth tho.

HAMLET. *(offstage)* Cock-a-doodle-doo! Cock-a-doodle-doo!

CLAUDIUS. *(Sits up.)* You're right. It doth tho. Boy, that was a fast night. *(He gets up and goes to the window.)* Who am I to argue with a rooster? *(He pulls back the drapes.)*

(HAMLET is sitting on the window-sill, crowing.)

HAMLET. Cock-a-doodle-doo!
CLAUDIUS. *(suspiciously)* There's something bothering that boy.

(Blackout. Lights up. CLAUDIUS and GERTRUDE are reading books on their thrones. It is another day.)

CLAUDIUS. Darling.
GERTRUDE. What, Dear?
CLAUDIUS. I'm really worried about our son.
GERTRUDE. Hamlet?
CLAUDIUS. He's not acting right lately.
GERTRUDE. Really?
CLAUDIUS. He seems so childish, so immature. He seems to have regressed.

(HAMLET enters the room singing a popular children's song or nursery rhyme and playing the child. He produces a hand puppet, possibly The Cookie Monster.)

HAMLET. Hello, Cookie Monster ... Hello, Hamlet.
Will you play with me? ... Do I have to?
It's my hand ... Let's play choo choo. *(exiting)*

Woo Woo ... Choo Choo
Woo Woo ... Choo Choo *(He exits.)*
GERTRUDE. *(a beat)* Regressed? In what way has Mommy's little angel regressed?
CLAUDIUS. I'm not sure. I just feel he has.

(Blackout. Lights up on Throne Room. CLAUDIUS is being briefed by POLONIUS.)

POLONIUS. At two-fifteen you address the Women's Literary Club of Copenhagen. At four-thirty you judge the Pig Contest at Elsinore State U. At six you have a candlelight dinner with the winner.
CLAUDIUS. I'm going to eat dinner with a pig?
POLONIUS. No, the winner is your dinner. The pig you invite is up to you.

(Suddenly HAMLET leaps out in front of them. With his back to the audience, he opens his cape wide.)

HAMLET. Aha!
POLONIUS. My Lord, he doth flash. *(HAMLET runs off.)*
CLAUDIUS. Polonius, for some reason I sense a deep hostility here.

BLACKOUT

Scene 6

A castle corridor. POLONIUS is at stage right. OPHELIA enters. She seems troubled. Her tummy is starting to protrude a little. She takes a few sniffs from a small inhaler.

OPHELIA. Woe is me! Woe is me! Woe is me!

POLONIUS. I hope this isn't going to be depressing. Okay, why woe is you?

OPHELIA. It's my Lord Hamlet. He seems out of sorts.

POLONIUS. I thought I forbade you to see him. Now what?

OPHELIA. He acted so strange, Father. I was sitting in my chamber snorting some... sorting some things, when in cometh he, his clothes all messed up, his stockings drooping down, his face white as a sheet, his knees knocking against each other...

POLONIUS. Maybe he saw the queen without her make-up.

OPHELIA. Nay, I think not. He was mumbling incoherent things, about incest and adultery, lust and lewdness, a foul and most unnatural deed and then he gave me this. *(She produces a letter.)*

POLONIUS. *(Takes letter.)* Let me see. *(Reads it.)* Yes, it is from Prince Hamlet. I can tell by the humor in his handwriting. He's the only one in the castle who crosses his "i"s. Aha! This is it. The answer to Hamlet's madness.

The King must hear of this immediately. Thanks loads, Ophelia. *(Starts out, then stops.)* By the way, you'd better cut down on sweets. You're starting to get a little big around the middle. Ta ta. *(He exits.)*

OPHELIA. *(to audience)* Woe is me! Woe is me! And one more Woe for the road. My lover, demented, my body four months wide with child and no date for New Year's Eve. You know it's amazing I'm so well adjusted.

BLACKOUT

Scene 7

The Throne Room. CLAUDIUS and GERTRUDE are seated.

BERNARDO. Presenting Rosencrantz and Guildenstern!

(ROSENCRANTZ and GUILDENSTERN enter. They both look like Groucho. During the following, they never stand still, moving around, sitting on laps, using props, etc.)

CLAUDIUS. Welcome, dear Rosencrantz and Guildenstern.
GERTRUDE. Or is it Guildenstern and Rosencrantz?
ROSENCRANTZ. It's Rosencrantz and Guildenstern for insurance.
GUILDENSTERN. And Guildenstern and Rosencrantz for accounting.

ROSENCRANTZ. And Rosencrantz and Guildenstern for business management.

GUILDENSTERN. And Wendell and Bruce for interior decorating.

ROSENCRANTZ. Now, what do you want to see? Something in accidental death or country French?

CLAUDIUS. No, Boys, no. Nothing like that today.

GUILDENSTERN. *(sitting on CLAUDIUS' lap)* Then what's on your mind, King C.? We haven't got all day.

CLAUDIUS. It's Hamlet. He's not acting normal.

ROSENCRANTZ. *(working a yo-yo)* Not normal. That's not normal.

CLAUDIUS. There's something bothering that kid and I want you to find out what.

ROSENCRANTZ. Detective work! Wonderful! That's where we shine. *(He takes out a rag and starts shining CLAUDIUS' shoes.)*

CLAUDIUS. You are two of his closest friends. He would never suspect you.

GUILDENSTERN. Wait a minute. We can't spy on a friend. It's *dis*gusting, *dis*honorable and *de*grading.

CLAUDIUS. How about a thousand ducats each?

GUILDENSTERN. And "de" way we make our living. You got a deal. When do we start?

CLAUDIUS. Immediately.

ROSENCRANTZ. I'm sorry. We'll have to start sooner. We're very busy people.

GUILDENSTERN. *(Holds out contract. To CLAUDIUS.)* Sign this contract and we're all set.

CLAUDIUS. Why do I have to sign? Don't you trust me?

ROSENCRANTZ. Depends. What line of work are you in?
CLAUDIUS. Politics.
ALL. Sign it! *(CLAUDIUS signs.)*
ROSENCRANTZ. All right, Claude, we're on the case.
GUILDENSTERN. Good.
ROSENCRANTZ. How about a raise?
CLAUDIUS. No!
GUILDENSTERN. How about Mondays off?
CLAUDIUS. No!
ROSENCRANTZ. How about a job for my Aunt Pauline?
CLAUDIUS. No!
ROSENCRANTZ. I'll be very honest with you. So far the job benefits stink. See you later, King. *(They exit.)*

(POLONIUS enters from the other direction.)

BERNARDO. *(announcing)* The Lord Chamberlain Polonius!
POLONIUS. *(Rushes in.)* Your Highness, I think I have the answer to Hamlet's lunacy.
GERTRUDE. Wonderful. Just don't blame it on us. We bought that boy everything. He wanted a cat, we bought him a cat. He wanted a dog, we bought him a dog. He wanted a dragon, we had Bernado pump air into the cat.
BERNARDO. What they didn't do for that boy.
GERTRUDE. I denied him nothing. And I mean nothing.
CLAUDIUS. That little wimp's got no reason to be acting so damn crazy.

POLONIUS. Ahhh, but he does because, you see, he is crazy, indeed crazy, absolutely crazy over my pure and chaste daughter, Ophelia.

CLAUDIUS. Pure and chaste, ha, ha, ha.

POLONIUS. You know her, Sir?

CLAUDIUS. Yes, but I'll deny it in court.

GERTRUDE. I don't believe it. Hamlet in love with another woman. Absurd.

CLAUDIUS. *(puzzled)* What do you mean another woman?

GERTRUDE. Ever read Oedipus?

CLAUDIUS. No.

GERTRUDE. Maybe it's better you don't.

POLONIUS. You see, I have forbidden her to see him, and naturally, it's driven him to poetic despair. *(opening the letter he took from OPHELIA)* Listen to this. *(reading)* Once upon a midnight dreary, while I pondered, weak and weary, over many a quaint and curious volume of forgotten lore, while I nodded, nearly napping, suddenly there came a tapping, as of someone gently rapping, rapping at my chamber door. Only this and nothing more.

CLAUDIUS. All right, hold it! Hold it! What muck! What absolute gibberish.

BERNARDO. Once upon a midnight dreary. What a cliche.

GERTRUDE. The money we wasted on private schools.

POLONIUS. Patience, my royalty. I'm getting to the good part. *(Continues reading.)* Eagerly I wished the morrow; vainly I had sought to borrow from my book surcease of sorrow — sorrow for the lost Lenore, nameless here for evermore.

GERTRUDE. Okay, who the hell is Lenore?

CLAUDIUS. Yes, and why is she nameless?

BERNARDO. It's obvious Hamlet's not playing with a full deck.

POLONIUS. Exactly, which is the surest sign he must be in love.

GERTRUDE. The little ingrate.

CLAUDIUS. I don't know. I'm just not convinced. Why am I so suspicious of that boy?

POLONIUS. If you need more proof, Sire, I have a plan. I will arrange a meeting between Hamlet and my daughter and you and I will conceal ourselves behind the drapes and peek-a-boo out.

CLAUDIUS. Voyeurism! I love it.

GERTRUDE. Can I watch, too?

POLONIUS. Sorry, my Lady. The house rules are just two at a time behind the drapes. Otherwise, there could be chaos.

CLAUDIUS. Let's be at it then. This is the moment when the evening light shines through the darkness and all answers are illuminated. Once and for all we shall discover whether there be method to Hamlet's madness or whether I'm making much ado about nothing. *(POLONIUS and GERTRUDE hiss him.)*

BLACKOUT

Scene 8

HAMLET is alone.

HAMLET. To be or not to be. That is the question. Do I get involved in this family domestic drivel, which could go on forever, or do I end it all by killing myself, which is really kind of stupid when you realize someday all of Denmark will be mine — which actually is another good reason for killing myself. But then if you kill yourself, how do you know things are any better on the other side? Suppose there's no Chinese food? What to do? What to do? And that dopey father of mine. Some kind of terrific father to have his only son commit murder for him. Boy, values in this country suck. Yay, I'm afraid in years to come people will think this tragic story a farce, and farce is what closes on Saturday night ... or is that satire?

(ROSENCRANTZ and GUILDENSTERN sneak up on him.)

ROSENCRANTZ and GUILDENSTERN. Chick-a-lickel! Chick-a-lickel! Chick-a-lickel-chell! All for Wittenberg, stand up and yell!
HAMLET. Hark! Me thinks I hear my school shout.
ROSENCRANTZ. It's us, Hamlet. Rosencrantz...
GUILDENSTERN. ...and Guildenstern.
HAMLET. Rosencrantz and Guildenstern, my two

college pals. What bringest thou to Denmark, dear friends?

ROSENCRANTZ. *(to GUILDENSTERN)* Don't tell him.

GUILDENSTERN. What do you mean, don't tell him?

ROSENCRANTZ. The King doesn't want him to know we're working for him.

HAMLET. Aha! You're working for the King!

ROSENCRANTZ. No, we're not working for the King. We're your friends. Why would we be working for the King? Who even mentioned we're working for the King?

GUILDENSTERN. I thought we were working for the King.

HAMLET. Aha! You're working for the King!

ROSENCRANTZ. What are you talking about? We're your friends. We wouldn't work for the King. *(to GUILDENSTERN)* Why would we work for the King?

GUILDENSTERN. He wants to find out what's making Hamlet crazy.

ROSENCRANTZ. *(to HAMLET)* What's making you crazy?

HAMLET. This conversation.

ROSENCRANTZ. We got it! Oh boy, wait till we tell the King.

HAMLET. Aha! You are working for the King!

ROSENCRANTZ. You know this is the most paranoid family I've had the displeasure of knowing.

HAMLET. Forgive me, dear sweet friends.

GUILDENSTERN. That's better. That's our old Hamlet talking.

HAMLET. Lately I haven't been myself.

ROSENCRANTZ. *(to GUILDENSTERN)* Take this down.

GUILDENSTERN. *(Takes out a steno pad and pencil.)* Shoot.

ROSENCRANTZ. Hasn't been himself. Split personality.

GUILDENSTERN. You talk to one, I'll talk to the other.

ROSENCRANTZ. Right. *(ROSENCRANTZ also takes out a steno pad and pencil.)*

HAMLET. I don't laugh any more.

ROSENCRANTZ and GUILDENSTERN. *(taking notes)* Laugh.

HAMLET. I don't joke.

ROSENCRANTZ and GUILDENSTERN. Joke.

HAMLET. I am plagued with suspicion, despair, and confusion.

ROSENCRANTZ and GUILDENSTERN. Confusion.

HAMLET. Even women no longer hold any interest for me. *(ROSENCRANTZ and GUILDENSTERN move away from him.)* My life has lost all meaning. My heart has lost all warmth. My emotions have been castrated.

GUILDENSTERN. That's it!

ROSENCRANTZ. What's it?

GUILDENSTERN. No balls! Hamlet has no balls. That's it in a nutshell.

ROSENCRANTZ. The King should be relieved to hear that.

GUILDENSTERN. Aha! We *are* working for the King!

ROSENCRANTZ. Hamlet, listen to me as a pal — No, better yet, as a friend — No, better yet, as a total stranger. You've got to snap out of this funk. Maybe you ought to get involved in more purposeful things.

HAMLET. Such as?

ROSENCRANTZ. Charities.

HAMLET. Charities? Nay! Charity for the poor is much too fattening. Every day there's a luncheon for the rich.

GUILDENSTERN. How about conservation? Maybe you can get people to stop pissing in the river and killing the frogs.

HAMLET. No. The peasants wouldn't like that. It's a Danish custom that goes back hundreds of years.

ROSENCRANTZ. Well, then, that leaves only one other thing. Community theatre.

GUILDENSTERN. You mean put on a play? What fun. We haven't done that for years.

ROSENCRANTZ. We'll charge three ducats for the orchestra, two guildings for the mezzanine and a farthing for the orange drink.

HAMLET. *(thinking deeply)* A play. A play might just be the thing.

GUILDENSTERN. Let's go for the teenage market. We'll do Romeo and Juliet.

HAMLET. No. Too silly.

ROSENCRANTZ. King Lear?

HAMLET. Soap opera.

GUILDENSTERN. Julius Caesar?

HAMLET. Dated.

ROSENCRANTZ. Othello?

HAMLET. Situation comedy.

GUILDENSTERN. Merchant of Venice?

HAMLET. Anti-semitic.

ROSENCRANTZ. Henry the Fourth, Henry the Fifth, Henry the Sixth, and Henry the Eighth.

HAMLET. The public's tired of sequels.

ROSENCRANTZ. Boy, nothing good seems to be coming out of the theatre anymore.

HAMLET. Okay, I'll tell you what. I'll go home and write my own play, and we'll put it on for the palace tomorrow night.

GUILDENSTERN. Tomorrow? Wonderful. I love to work under pressure. I'll make the costumes.

ROSENCRANTZ. I'll paint the sets, and we can rehearse in my father's barn.

HAMLET. It'll be something significant. Something arty.

GUILDENSTERN. Arty! Arty! That's what's killing show business. Nobody likes arty. The public stays away from arty.

HAMLET. I'll write something to catch the conscience of the King. Yes, that's it. The play's the thing. Once and for all, I will find out whether Claudius is the culprit or whether the ghost of my father has just been hosing me since Act One, Scene One.

ROSENCRANTZ. We'll pass out leaflets, put up posters and arrange for an opening-night party.

HAMLET. I'll go write the play.

GUILDENSTERN. And we'll go tell the King.

HAMLET. Aha! You're working for the King! *(He lunges at them and chases them off stage.)*

BLACKOUT

Scene 9

OPHELIA'S bedroom. Stage right. OPHELIA, sitting on a stool, is smoking a joint. She is showing further signs of pregnancy.

OPHELIA. Troubles. I'm adrift in a sea of troubles. But then who knows? Some people say cruises are fun.

(There is a knock at the door.)

POLONIUS. *(off)* Ophelia, it's your father and King Claudius. *(OPHELIA quickly puts out her joint and tries to clear the air.)*

(POLONIUS and CLAUDIUS enter.)

POLONIUS. Do you smell something sweet?
CLAUDIUS. *(sniffs)* Yes. She must use the same toilet water as my musicians.
OPHELIA. My Lord. Your Highness.
CLAUDIUS. Hello, Ophelia. Say, you're putting on a little weight around the middle, aren't you?
OPHELIA. Lately I've had a craving for icecream and pickles at two in the morning. To what do I attribute the honor of this visit, my Lord?
POLONIUS. Ophelia, King Claudius needs your help. He is trying to pinpoint the reason for Hamlet's mad-

ness, and I have assured him that it's simply because he's mad for you.

CLAUDIUS. I have heard that on many an occasion the young Prince takes a short-cut to his room by going through your room. Is that not so?

OPHELIA. Well, yes, that's true. But so do a lot of guys. I'm centrally located.

CLAUDIUS. Nevertheless, if indeed my stepson's madness be over you, then I'm prepared to announce a royal nuptial and award you both a set of high grade luggage and two tickets out of town.

OPHELIA. I'd love to go to Turkey. I understand the poppies there are something else.

POLONIUS. My daughter has always been into plants.

(There is a knock at the door.)

CLAUDIUS. That must be Hamlet. We will conceal ourselves behind these drapes.

POLONIUS. There's nothing I love better than peeping.
(POLONIUS and CLAUDIUS hide behind a set of drapes.)

OPHELIA. If I could marry Prince Hamlet, it would solve so many of my problems. I'll be a wonderful wife to him, and we'll be so happy together. Mr. and Mrs. Hamlet ... *(pats tummy)* ... and family. We'll live in a little white castle with a picket moat and in the mornings we'll hold hands and go for walks and in the afternoons I'll pack lunches and we'll go on picnics and in the evenings we'll sit by the fire and he'll read his books and I'll smoke my pipe because let's face it, without the pipe I couldn't possibly endure such a dismal existence.

(ROSENCRANTZ and GUILDENSTERN enter.)

ROSENCRANTZ. Hi, we'd like to hang up a poster for a play we're putting on tomorrow. I understand there's a lot of traffic through this room.
GUILDENSTERN. I have a ticket for front row center if you're interested in sitting on my lap.
ROSENCRANTZ. Sit on my lap and you can see it from the balcony.
GUILDENSTERN. Naughty, Naughty!

(They nuge each other playfully. There is a knock on the door.)

OPHELIA. Quick, hide. It's Hamlet.
ROSENCRANTZ. Hamlet? Why should we hide from Hamlet?
OPHELIA. Just hide or you'll ruin the chance of my lifetime.
GUILDENSTERN. We're hiding. *(They go to where CLAUDIUS and POLONIUS are standing.)*
CLAUDIUS. Find your own place. *(ROSENCRANTZ goes to another set of drapes.)*
ROSENCRANTZ. Behind these.
GUILDENSTERN. Right.

(They hide behind the drapes. FRANCISCO enters.)

FRANCISCO. Hi, I'm sorry I'm late. I had guard duty.
OPHELIA. Oh, no, Francisco! I forgot about you.

(Just then there's another knock.)

OPHELIA. Quick, hide. It's Hamlet.
FRANCISCO. Oh, oh! *(FRANCISCO desperately searches for a hiding place. He tries behind both drapes, but they're taken.)* Sorry. Sorry.
OPHELIA. Under the bed.
FRANCISCO. Right.

(FRANCISCO dives under an imaginary bed. HORATIO enters.)

HORATIO. Hi, I thought I'd drop by a little early today.
OPHELIA. Horatio. You had a two-thirty. I've got to get an appointment book.

(There's another knock.)

OPHELIA. Quick, hide. It's Hamlet.
HORATIO. Right. *(He rushes to the drapes and under the bed. All taken.)*
OPHELIA. In the trunk! In the trunk!
HORATIO. Right.

(HORATIO climbs into an imaginary trunk. BERNARDO enters, holding two heads on sticks. He does all the voices.)

OPHELIA. Oh, no. The Three Musketeers.
VOICES. *(ATHOS)* All for one and one for all.
VOICES. *(PORTHOS)* That's how we did it last time.

(There is another knock.)

OPHELIA. Hide! It's Hamlet. *(THE THREE MUS-KETEERS search frantically for a place to hide.)*
VOICES. *(ATHOS)* Where?
VOICES. *(PORTHOS)* The armoire!
VOICES. *(ARAMIS)* Good idea.

(THE THREE MUSKETEERS climb into an imaginary armoire. OPHELIA fixes her hair as HAMLET enters.)

OPHELIA. My Prince. Come in. *(HAMLET enters, perfectly oblivious to all the bodies on the stage.)*
HAMLET. *(mumbling)* To be or not to be. That is the question.
OPHELIA. What was the question?
HAMLET. To be or ot to be. It keeps sticking in my mind. It's not that literate a phrase but somehow it seems important. Am I really thinking about suicide? Why would I commit suicide? I'm a big shot prince. I'm putting on a play, I drive a fine horse, he's hardly ever in the shop ... Then why do I keep remembering those stupid lines? I'm so confused. Ophelia, can I level with you? There's something rotten in Denmark.
OPHELIA. Really? Maybe it's all the dead frogs in the river.
HAMLET. *(laying his head on her lap.)* Nay. 'Tis deeper, 'tis darker, 'tis more disagreeable, 'tis you have a spare tire around your tummy? *(raises head)* Ophelia, you haven't been fooling around, have you?
OPHELIA. Of course I haven't, my Prince. *(All in the room start to giggle.)*
HAMLET. *(rising)* Ophelia, I sense we are not alone.

OPHELIA. I'm worried about you, my Lord. Your noble mind has become so suspicious of late. Of course we're alone, my Prince. *(HAMLET goes to the drapes, takes a beat and quickly pulls them aside. CLAUDIUS and POLONIUS stand there, motionless.)*

HAMLET. Oh, yeah? Who be this then?

OPHELIA. Who be what when?

HAMLET. Be this not the King and Polonius, your father?

OPHELIA. Nay, be not silly. 'Tis no one, my young monarch.

HAMLET. You see no one?

OPHELIA. No one. *(HAMLET then pulls back the other drapes, revealing GUILDENSTERN and ROSENCRANTZ.)*

HAMLET. And be this not Rosencrantz and Guildenstern?

OPHELIA. Of course not, There is no one, my beloved Majesty.

HAMLET. No one? *(pointing to FRANCISCO)* How about under the bed? Be this not the soldier, Francisco?

OPHELIA. Absolutely not, my sweet Dane of depression.

HAMLET. *(pointing to HORATIO)* And in the trunk? Be this not Horatio? *(HORATIO looks up and shakes his head "no.")*

HAMLET. No?

OPHELIA. I guess not.

HAMLET. How about in this armoire? Be this not the... the...

OPHELIA. The Three Musketeers?

HAMLET. Yes!

OPHELIA. No.

HAMLET. *(sits down dejected)* What's wrong with me, Ophelia? Lately I just don't trust anyone. The King, the Queen, your Father, the Sheriff of Nottingham ...

OPHELIA. Hamlet, let's get down to the nitty gritty. Would you like to marry me?

HAMLET. No.

OPHELIA. Okay, maybe I moved too fast. What about going steady?

HAMLET. Can't.

OPHELIA. What if I put you down for a three-fifteen on Wednesday?

HAMLET. Ophelia, my love, I just stopped by to say that until I fulfill a promise to a certain dead person who was once married to my Mommy, you're going to have to start taking a lot of cold showers. But after the play tomorrow night, a number of questions that have no answers will need answers nevermore. *(He starts out, then stops.)* By the way, there's a great new place in town called "The Nunnery". You ought to get thee there. *(Passing THE THREE MUSKETEERS)* So long, boys.

ALL. See ya.

(He exits. Everyone comes out of hiding. As they speak they put their arm around the shoulders of the last speaker, forming a straight line facing the audience.)

OPHELIA. Why are men so complicated?

CLAUDIUS. There is trouble afoot. Any fool can see that.

POLONIUS. A foreboding of evil.

FRANCISCO. Treachery and deception.
BERNARDO. Anguish and bewilderment.
GUILDENSTERN. Knavery and heartless cruelty.
ROSENCRANTZ. Coldblooded and barbarous brutality.

The GHOST enters.)

GHOST. And this is only the end of Act One. See you in twelve minutes, folks.

CURTAIN

END OF ACT I

ACT II
Scene 1

The Throne Room. BERNARDO is hawking souvenirs and refreshments from a tray.

BERNARDO. Programs! Programs! Get your souvenir programs! Refreshments! You can't enjoy theatre on an empty stomach.

(ROSENCRANTZ approaches BERNARDO.)

ROSENCRANTZ. Do you have any Juju Bees?
BERNARDO. No Juju Bees.
ROSENCRANTZ. Any Milk Duds?
BERNARDO. No Milk Duds.
ROSENCRANTZ. What do you have that's sweet?
BERNARDO. Just the Stage Manager. *(He exits.)*
ROSENCRANTZ. It's this sort of repartee that's killing the theatre. *(He exits.)*

(CLAUDIUS, GERTRUDE, and POLONIUS enter.)

CLAUDIUS. Sixteen ducats a ticket. You'd think being parents of the playwright we could get freebies.
GERTRUDE. It's your own fault. You wouldn't invest in the play.
CLAUDIUS. Invest in a play? I'm a King, not a moron.

(They sit.)

POLONIUS. I heard the Prince couldn't make up his mind whether to make it a comedy or a drama, to give it a happy ending or a sad ending, to use his real name or a phony name ... Mark my word, no good can come of wishy-washiness.

CLAUDIUS. Maybe yes, maybe no.

POLONIUS. *(pinching the King's cheek)* Of course. Why couldn't I think of that.

(The GHOST enters.)

GHOST. Such a big production for one lousy murder. He's got no time to kill his uncle, but he's got plenty of time to write a play. *(He sits.)*

(HAMLET enters to Stage Left.)

HAMLET. Okay, everyone, get ready, the show starts in five minutes.

(GUILDENSTERN approaches HAMLET.)

GUILDENSTERN. Excuse me, Prince. Rosencrantz is in his room crying. The opening night telegrams got him down. Listen to these. *(going through telegrams)* "Eat shit!" "Eat shit!" "Eat shit!" "Eat shit!"

HAMLET. You know nothing about theatre lore, do you, Guildenstern? "Eat shit" is Portugese for "Good Luck".

GUILDENSTERN. No kidding? I wonder how they say "Merry Christmas"?

(He goes off just as HORATIO and OPHELIA approach.)

HORATIO. Hamlet! Hamlet! The leading lady is dead.
HAMLET. Another opening night tradition.
HORATIO. She choked to death on a herring bone.
HAMLET. Why would she eat a man's suit?
HORATIO. No, a real herring bone. Someone sent her a fish in the mail.
HAMLET. Alas, all is lost.
OPHELIA. No so, my Lord. I know the part.
HAMLET. How could you? You haven't even read it.
OPHELIA. It doesn't matter, as long as one believes in the magic of theatre.
HORATIO. Let her do it, Hamlet. Otherwise, we'll have to refund everyone's money which we already spent on soap for the john.
HAMLET. Damn it, I'm going to play a hunch. Ophelia, you've got the part.
OPHELIA. Show business is all luck, isn't it?
HAMLET. That's what they say. *(OPHELIA and HORATIO exit.)*
HAMLET. *(calling)* Francisco!

(FRANCISCO enters.)

FRANCISCO. My Lord?
HAMLET. During the performance I want you to keep an eye on Claudius.
FRANCISCO. Right.
HAMLET. And keep an eye on Polonius.
FRANCISCO. Right.

HAMLET. And keep an eye on Gertrude.
FRANCISCO. Right.
HAMLET. And keep an eye on my hat and coat. Actors are a deperate lot.
CLAUDIUS. *(impatient, whistling)* Come on! Let's go!
POLONIUS. On with the show!
GERTRUDE. Showtime! Showtime!
HAMLET. Okay everybody! Places! Places! Places! Curtain going up! Music! Lights! Overture! Take it, Bernardo.

(BERNARDO enters.)

BERNARDO.
CLAP YOUR HANDS, STAMP YOUR FEET.
TO OPEN THE SHOW WE'VE GOT A TREAT.
LORDS, AND LADIES, KING AND QUEEN,
YOU AIN'T GOT NOTHIN' IF YOU AIN'T
   GOT SWING.

(OPHELIA, ROSENCRANTZ and GUILDENSTERN enter and sing the following song, a la Peggy Lee's "Fever".)

OPHELIA, ROSENCRANTZ and GUILDENSTERN. *(singing)*
DOUBLE, DOUBLE, TOIL AND TROUBLE
FIRE BURN AND CAULDRON BUBBLE
EYE OF NEWT, AND TOE OF FROG,
WOOL OF BAT, AND TONGUE OF DOG.
FINGER OF BIRTH-STRANGLED BABE,
DITCH-DELIVERED BY A DRAB.
BY THE PRICKING OF MY THUMBS,

SOMETHING WICKED THIS WAY COMES.
DOUBLE, DOUBLE, TOIL AND TROUBLE
FIRE BURN AND CAULDRON BUBBLE ...
OUT OUT, DAMN SPOT.
OUT, OUT, DAMN SPOT OUT!

(The spotlight goes out and they are greeted by bravos and wild applause.)

CLAUDIUS. Hot Stuff! Bravo!
GERTRUDE. A hit. The show's a hit! *(OPHELIA runs to HAMLET.)*
OPHELIA. I'm a star, Hamlet. A star! And with my own nose. *(She exits.)*
ROSENCRANTZ. *(to HAMLET)* We'll talk to you in the morning about a new contract and a bigger dressing room.
GUILDENSTERN. You're on next, Hamlet. Eat shit!
HAMLET. Thanks.
BERNARDO. And now, on a more serious note, here's Prince Hamlet with a poem he wrote. *(Only GERTRUDE applauds.)*
HAMLET. Thank you. Thank you, Mother. *(He begins.)*
Roses are red, violets are blue,
There was this great King, too old to screw.
CLAUDIUS. Oh, smut. I love it.
HAMLET.
There was the Queen who found it frustrating,
And so the King's brother she started dating.
CLAUDIUS. The kid's a fruitcake. But he sure knows

how to rhyme.
HAMLET. The brother, not satisfied with merely lust, decided that the King must bite the dust.
CLAUDIUS. *(concerned)* This sounds familiar.
GERTRUDE. Maybe it's an old classic, plagiarized.
HAMLET.
Wanting the crown alone to wear,
He poisoned the King right in his ear.
CLAUDIUS. *(angry, rising)* Lights! Lights!

(The audience stirs.)

POLONIUS. Oh, oh. Trouble.
GERTRUDE. What's wrong, my Lord?
CLAUDIUS. This show sucks!
HAMLET. Look who's calling himself a critic now.
CLAUDIUS. As King and owner of all the beach front property, I'm cancelling the show and going home. Come on, everyone. Follow me. *(He points his finger and marches off. All but GERTRUDE follow.)*
GERTRUDE. *(to HAMLET)* It's kids like you that make a second marriage so difficult. *(She exits.)*

(HORATIO enters.)

HAMLET. *(overjoyed)* We did it, Horatio, we did it!
HORATIO. We did nothing but put a bunch of hard-working kids with stars in their eyes out of work.
HAMLET. But at last I know my uncle is guilty. There's no doubt about it. And now to avenge my father.
GHOST. Now you're talking.

HORATIO. Oh, screw your father. I'd rather be in a hit show. Boy, you really are infantile. You have this terrible hangup about getting even. *(He exits.)*

HAMLET. I thought I was being very Shapespearean.

(POLONIUS enters.)

POLONIUS. Oh, boy, Hamlet, are you in trouble. The Queen wants to see you right away. I haven't seen her this upset since you put a porcupine in the King's armour.

HAMLET. Be gone, ye olde fart. *(POLONIUS exits.)*

(The following enter and exit quickly.)

FRANCISCO. Dope!
BERNARDO. Jerk!
ROSENCRANTZ. Ninny!
GUILDENSTERN. Airhead!

(OPHELIA approaches.)

OPHELIA. You're really a spoiled brat. For a minute there I really had something going with my life, but leave it to you to screw things up. Eat shit!

HAMLET. Gee, thanks. *(OPHELIA exits.)*

HAMLET. This is one of those horrifying times, when one feels that although he has chosen the right path, done the noble deed, his friends nevertheless turn their backs on him, allowing this great moment of triumph to come crashing into dust. On the other hand, I've got to be realistic. We didn't have many theatre parties lined up, anyway.

BLACKOUT

Scene 2

CLAUDIUS' chambers (Stage Center). KING CLAUDIUS is at prayer.

CLAUDIUS. Dear God, If ever you loved me, then please help me get rid of that dipstick, Hamlet. I'll do anything. I'll even obey a few of your commandments.

(POLONIUS enters.)

POLONIUS. Excuse me, your Highness.
CLAUDIUS. Please, I'm trying to get nearer my God than thee.
POLONIUS. Sorry to interrupt you, my Lord, but I thought you might be interested in learning that the Queen has sent for her son.
CLAUDIUS. That dirty, suspicious little cocker. *(looking up)* Not you, God. Hamlet.
POLONIUS. What I shall do, my Lord, is hide myself behind her drapes and do more peeping. I love peeping. Not many people my age can do peeping.

CLAUDIUS. Go, good Polonius. We must find out what that little troublemaker is up to.

POLONIUS. See ya! *(He exits.)*

CLAUDIUS. It dost warm my heart to know I am not the only lowlife sneak in Denmark. *(back to praying)* Okay, God, back to you. Now, here's my list for tonight. I would like a bigger summer house, a book of familiar quotations, a new pair of hockey skates, a box of chocolates, some gum ...

(HAMLET approaches and sees CLAUDIUS at prayer. He draws his sword.)

HAMLET. Now might I do it? Nay, not while he's praying. What if God is fooled into believing he's a saintly one and he's sent to Heaven? Poor God. How easily he's taken in by religion. No, I shall wait to catch the King in a less holy position. Hopefully, while he's running naked among the sheep. *(He starts out.)*

BLACKOUT

Scene 3

GERTRUDE'S chambers. She is pacing around the room and smoking a cigarette a la Bette Davis. HAMLET enters.

HAMLET. You sent for me, Mommy Dearest?

GERTRUDE. Don't you Mommy Dearest me, you little rascal. I've been doing a lot of thinking. I know what's on your mind.

(POLONIUS sneaks in across the back of the room and hides behind the drapes.)

HAMLET. What speakest you, Mother?

GERTRUDE. All this nonsense about not wanting to call Claudius "daddy". You hate him, don't you?

HAMLET. Yes, of course, I hate him. I loathe him. I despise him.

GERTRUDE. Of course you do. And you know why? Because you love me.

HAMLET. Of course, I love you, Mother.

GERTRUDE. But it's not just a regular love, it's a sick love, isn't it? A real sick perverted love, isn't it?

HAMLET. No, not too perverted. You know, a regular mother and son love.

GERTRUDE. Don't give me that, you filthy minded thing. Say it out loud. Tell me how you feel. If you can't have me, then no one can. Go ahead, you wild and crazy guy, say it

HAMLET. I hate him! I hate him! I hate him!

GERTRUDE. Good, get it out of your system, Mama's little man.

HAMLET. I'd like to rip his eyes out, tear his flesh apart.

GERTRUDE. More ! More!

HAMLET. I'd like to smash his teeth.

GERTRUDE. You want to see me in a bathing suit, my

love? It'll just take a minute.

HAMLET. *(Grabbing GERTRUDE by the shoulders.)* He's a cad, he's a swine. When I think of you in his bed ...

GERTRUDE. Not too rough. Not too rough.

HAMLET. The lust! The incestuous lust ...

GERTRUDE. *(Breathing heavily.)* Don't stop! Don't stop!

HAMLET. *(Drawing his sword.)* I'd love to run him through, you hear me? Rip his guts right out ...

GERTRUDE. Such passion. Such raw, savage, sweaty passion. I love it. *(HAMLET begins thrusting his sword about the room and finally into the drapes.)*

HAMLET. Take this and this and this and this.

GERTRUDE. *(Her eyes closed in ecstasy.)* Thrust, son! Thrust! Thrust! Thrust!

(As HAMLET thrusts through the drapes, we hear a loud moan from POLONIUS.)

POLONIUS. AAAAAAaaaaaaaaaaaahhhhhhhhhhhhh!

GERTRUDE. Was that me? Wow, such rapture. *(POLONIUS staggers out from the drapes and slumps to the floor.)*

HAMLET. It's Polonius. I stabbed Polonius.

POLONIUS. I am dying. It hurts like the dickens. *(He dies.)*

GERTRUDE. You've killed Polonius. How felonious.

HAMLET. Yes, my good mother. Almost as horrible as a brother killing a King and marrying his wife. Why, Mother, why? *(He approaches GERTRUDE threateningly.)*

GERTRUDE. Please, you forget how cold the winters are here in Denmark.

(The GHOST appears. He bends over and looks at POLONIUS.)

GHOST. Oh, Christ, did you do this? You got the wrong guy.

HAMLET. I know, I know.

GHOST. What's the matter with you? Can't you do anything right anymore.

HAMLET. Hey, Too err is human, to forgive divine.

GERTRUDE. *(puzzled)* Who are you talking to?

HAMLET. To the ghost of my father. The ghost of your former husband. Don't you see him? Don't you see the pain in his face? The hurt in his eyes your adultery has caused him? Don't you see the torture in his brow? The torment in his veins?

GHOST. Up until now I thought I was fairly cute.

GERTRUDE. *(Backing off from HAMLET in fright.)* He's mad. Oh, my poor son. That he is mad, 'tis true, 'tis true; 'tis pity and pity 'tis, 'tis true. *(GERTRUDE runs out of the room.)*

HAMLET. Gee, I hope I haven't upset Mom. *(He sits down, dejected.)*

GHOST. *(Looking down at the dead POLONIUS.)* Poor Polonius. Boy, you're really up a creek now, Hamlet. To kill the father of the girl you wanted to marry ... That's heavy. *(He sits next to HAMLET and puts his arm around him.)*

HAMLET. I know. Now who am I going to get to pay for the wedding?

BLACKOUT

Scene 4

CLAUDIUS' chambers. CLAUDIUS is is still at prayer. He has a shopping bag filled with beautifully wrapped gifts next to him.

CLAUDIUS. ... some salt water taffy, a jar of grape jelly, a deck of cards with five aces.

(ROSENCRANTZ and GUILDENSTERN enter.)

ROSENCRANTZ. You sent for us, Claude?
GUILDENSTERN. *(Indicating shopping bag.)* Hey, presents!
CLAUDIUS. They're mine. I prayed for them, I got them. Look, I've got to do something about that lunatic stepson of mine. Have you two any suggestions?
GUILDENSTERN. I don't know. What do you suggest, Rosencrantz?
ROSENCRANTZ. I don't know. What do you suggest, Claudius?
CLAUDIUS. I don't know. That's why I'm asking you.
ROSENCRANTZ. Well, I suggest you better come up with a better suggestion than that.

(GERTRUDE rushes in.)

GERTRUDE. Claudius, there's something rotten in Denmark.
GUILDENSTERN. Have you checked the gymnasium?
GERTRUDE. Hamlet has slain Polonius.
ROSENCRANTZ. Ahhh, then maybe it's Polonius that's rotten in Denmark.
CLAUDIUS. *(outraged)* That boy ... That boy ... that does it. This time he's gone too far. You do not kill a Lord

Chamberlain in this town without at least saying you're sorry.

GUILDENSTERN. That's right There is such a thing as common decency, even in Denmark.

CLAUDIUS. Right! Come on, Boys.

GERTRUDE. Where are you going?

CLAUDIUS. To finally handle things my way.

GERTRUDE. Please, Claudius, he's a very sensitive child. Try to be kind to him.

CLAUDIUS. At times, my dear lady, you must be cruel to be kind. *(CLAUDIUS, ROSENCRANTZ & GUILDENSTERN exit.)*

GERTRUDE. *(puzzled)* Cruel to be kind? Sometimes it's better not to question those kind of lines.

BLACKOUT

Scene 5

HAMLET'S room. HAMLET paces in front of a large door.

HAMLET. To be or not to be, that is the question. Whether I should try to pin the murder of Polonius on someone else or take the rap myself. I probably need a good lawyer, but they're all too busy with real estate deals where the big bucks are. What to do? What to do?

(There is a knock at the door.)

HAMLET. Yes. Who's there?

(A voice is heard from behind the door.)

VOICE. Message for Prince Hamlet.
HAMLET. Coming *(Going to door and then turning to audience.)* To tip or not to tip? Do I give him a quince or a guilding? A danker or a farthing? Maybe a deutchmark would be enough, but then why would I tip in German money? There are so many things that need answering.

(CLAUDIUS, ROSENCRANTZ and GUILDENSTERN enter and sneak behind HAMLET. CLAUDIUS pulls out a club and brings it down on HAMLET'S head. HAMLET slumps to the ground.)

GUILDENSTERN. Boy, you sure pack a nice punch for a white collar person.
CLAUDIUS. Thank you. I was head-bashing champ at summer camp. *(Hands a letter to ROSENCRANTZ.)* Okay, I've arranged for a ship to take you and Hamlet to England. When you get there, you will hand this letter and Prince Hamlet to the authorities. *(Hands him the tickets.)* Here are your tickets.
GUILDENSTERN. Thanks.
ROSENCRANTZ. Wait a minute, King. Ours are round-trip and Hamlet's is only one way.
CLAUDIUS. *(Smiles evilly.)* That's right.
ROSENCRANTZ & GUILDENSTERN. *(Getting the idea.)* Ooooooooohhhhhhhhh!

BLACKOUT

Scene 6

*The Throne Room. Several days later. CLAUDIUS and GER-
TRUDE are seated. CLAUDIUS is getting a haircut from
BERNARDO.*

CLAUDIUS. This is the life. This is the way being a King was meant to be. My marriage is going good. I'm putting away a few dollars every month. I'm content. Hamlet was the trouble-maker.
GERTRUDE. Children, children, children. When they're young, they step on your feet, and when they're old they step on your hearts.
CLAUDIUS. *(Looks at her for a beat.)* You're so Jewish, sometimes.

(OPHELIA enters singing and passsing out stems from a marijuana plant. Her clothes are dirty, her hair is frizzed, and she's in her fifth month.)

OPHELIA.
ROLL ME OVER IN THE CLOVER,
ROLL ME OVER, LAY ME DOWN AND DO IT AGAIN.
CLAUDIUS. Yes, things are going well for everyone, except maybe poor Ophelia.
GERTRUDE. Yes, poor tyke. Mad as a hoot owl.
CLAUDIUS. A hoot owl, is it? I never knew they were mad.
GERTRUDE. Yes. Hoot owls, road runners, daffy ducks,

the lot. All mad.

OPHELIA. *(sings)*

OH, THIS IS NUMBER ONE AND THE FUN HAS JUST BEGUN,

ROLL ME OVER, LAY ME DOWN AND DO IT AGAIN.

BERNARDO. *(Holding a mirror to the King and speaking with Italian accent.)* How'sa this boss?

CLAUDIUS. A little more on the side. I'd like to get that devilish look.

BERNARDO. Gotcha.

OPHELIA. *(sings)*

OH, THIS IS NUMBER TWO, NOW I'LL DO IT TO YOU

ROLL ME OVER, LAY ME DOWN AND DO IT AGAIN.

(OPHELIA hands some plants to CLAUDIUS and GERTRUDE.)

CLAUDIUS. What manner of plant is this she passeth out?

GERTRUDE. An herb, I believe, supposed to give brownies a special zest all their own.

CLAUDIUS. *(Shakes his head.)* Ophelia mad. Hamlet mad. Mental health in this country is going into the crapper.

OPHELIA. *(sings)*

OH, THIS IS NUMBER THREE, NUMBER THREE I DO FOR FREE

ROLL ME OVER, LAY ME DOWN AND DO IT AGAIN.

(She exits.)

CLAUDIUS. Brave girl. Very brave girl.
GERTRUDE. A bit chunky, but I guess when you're bananas, it doesn't matter much.

(There is the sound of a scuffle outside the throne room.)

CLAUDIUS. What the hell's going on out there?

(LAERTES enters, sword in hand.)

LAERTES. It is I, Laertes, back from France to avenge the death of my father, Polonius.
CLAUDIUS. That's just what I need. Another kid in town who wants to avenge his father.
LAERTES. An eye for an eye, a tooth for a tooth.
CLAUDIUS. That seems reasonable enough.
LAERTES. A life for a life.
CLAUDIUS. No deal!
LAERTES. *(His sword at the King's neck.)* Say your prayers, King Claudius.
CLAUDIUS. Why? I don't need anything.
LAERTES. Then fare thee well. I'm running you through.
GERTRUDE. Thank God I still have my black dress.
CLAUDIUS. Wait! Wait! Don't kill me. It wasn't I who killed your father. It was Hamlet.
LAERTES. Hamlet, the noble Prince of Denmark? That sweet, kind, gentle great Dane? Prince Hamlet, fair of face, warm of heart, who never paid a lick of attention to me in his whole life—killed my father?
CLAUDIUS. *(Putting his arm around LAERTES, he walks him to*

a corner of the room away from listening ears.) Come over here.

LAERTES. What? What?

CLAUDIUS. Can you keep a secret?

LAERTES. Did you hear about me and the Duke of Chablis?

CLAUDIUS. No.

LAERTES. See. I didn't tell anyone.

CLAUDIUS. I sent Hamlet to England with a letter instructing them to put him to death immediately, if not sooner.

LAERTES. Then I am avenged?

CLAUDIUS. Of course. All's well that ends well. There's absolutely nothing else you've got to be pissed about.

(OPHELIA enters again.)

OPHELIA. *(sings)*
OH, THIS IS NUMBER NINE,
PLEASE DO IT ONE MORE TIME.
ROLL ME OVER, LAY ME DOWN AND DO IT
 AGAIN.
(LAERTES stares at CLAUDIUS.)
CLAUDIUS. Well, almost absolutely nothing.

BLACKOUT

Scene 7

A ship's deck. (Stage Right) It is very foggy. ROSENCRANTZ is peering desperately through a telescope. GUILDENSTERN is at his side.

ROSENCRANTZ. Forty days we've been at sea and still no sight of England. I'm worried, really worried.
GUILDENSTERN. I don't want to alarm you, but the crew is talking mutiny.
ROSENCRANTZ. It's the captain's fault. He never should have cancelled the Saturday night dance.
GUILDENSTERN. He was angry. None of the men wanted to be his date.

(HAMLET approaches holding his head in pain.)

HAMLET. Ooooh, my head. What hit me? I last remember going to the door for a telegram. To tip or not to tip. I must not have tipped.
GUILDENSTERN. Bad news, Prince. Forty days we've been at sea and still no sight of England. We're out of food, we're out of water ...
HAMLET. What about stationery?
GUILDENSTERN. We've got stationery.
HAMLET. Good. Let's write for help.
ROSENCRANTZ. I'm afraid, Prince Hamlet, there's no hope for survival.
HAMLET. No hope?
ROSENCRANTZ. Less than that.
HAMLET. Oh, that this sad, sad mortal should never

know that moment of tranquil contentment ... I am a prince. Hath not a prince eyes, hands, senses, passions? If you prick us, do we not bleed? If you tickle us, do we not laugh?

GUILDENSTERN. Is this gonna be long?

HAMLET. I'm afraid so.

ROSENCRANTZ. I just feel sorry for the kids who are gonna have to memorize this in school. *(They exit.)*

HAMLET. To die, to sleep, perchance to dream. Aye, there's the rub. What a fool I've been. Why couldn't I see how nice I had it. Ophelia, a girl who loved me. Queen Gertrude, an easy-going, happy-go-lucky mother. Claudius, a stepfather who hardly hit me. I gave it up for what? Principle? Nay, immaturity. And now it's all gone and I'm going to die like a whimpering dog on a sea with no trees. What a brilliant analogy.

(He sees a light in the distance.)

HAMLET. But soft. I think I see a light. What goes there? *(The light comes closer towards the boat. It is the GHOST with a lantern.)*

GHOST. It's me, Hamlet.

HAMLET. Father. What are you doing out here on the high seas?

GHOST. There's a reason you haven't reached England yet. Your boat is still tied to the dock.

HAMLET. I'm saved! I'm saved! You hear that everyone? I'm saved. And I'm going home. Home to Elsinore where from now on everything is going to be peaches and cream and I'm going to live happily ever after and then

some. *(He exits.)*
GHOST. You can tell he doesn't know this story.

BLACKOUT

Scene 8

A graveyard. (Stage Left) A GRAVEDIGGER is digging.

GRAVEDIGGER. *(singing)*
A MAID AND A CURSED PRINCE WENT A WOOING ONE DAY
SAID THE MAID TO THE CURSED PRINCE, YOU MAY HAVE YOUR WAY.
THE CURSE WAS SOON BROKEN. THEY MADE LOVE IN THE ROAD,
AND THEN THE CURSED PRINCE TURNED BACK INTO A TOAD,
SINGING NONNIE, NONNIE, NONNIE AND A RING-A-DING-DING,
AND A HEY AND A NONNIE AND A PONG AND A PING.
(HAMLET approaches.)
HAMLET. *(inhaling)* Ahh, I'm getting near home. I can almost smell the stagnant sewage in the moat. *(He spots the gravedigger.)* Lo! What doest thou?
GRAVEDIGGER. What thinkest I doest? I diggest.

HAMLET. Then what diggest thou then for?

GRAVEDIGGER. What thinkest I diggest for, stupidest?

HAMLET. Lo! A riddlest! I love a riddlest. Let me guesseth. Thou diggest for potatoes.

GRAVEDIGGER. Nope.

HAMLET. I need a hint. Is it bigger than a leg of lamb?

GRAVEDIGGER. What do you think you diggest in a graveyard, dum dum? *(He throws a skull to HAMLET.)*

HAMLET. *(thinking)* Hmmm! Dum dum. I've got it! A grave? Of course. I knew I'd get it. *(Studying the skull.)* This head. I seem to have known it once.

GRAVEDIGGER. Oh, come on. You must know who that is.

HAMLET. Was.

GRAVEDIGGER. That's Henny Yorick, the King's former stand-up comic.

HAMLET. Yorick? This was Henny Yorick? Alas, poor Yorick. I knew him well.

GRAVEDIGGER. My wife and I loved him. He was class.

HAMLET. You're telling me. Who canst forget such brilliance as "Taketh my wife, please!"

GRAVEDIGGER. Or, "My best friend ran away with my wife and let me tell you, I miss him." *(The two are laughing hysterically.)* He was certainly good with one-liners.

HAMLET. Like they say, brevity is the soul of wit.

GRAVEDIGGER. You know my favorite one was "My wife once told me, 'I love you terribly' and I said 'You certainly do.' "

HAMLET. Remember "My wife's on a diet. Coconuts

and bananas. She hasn't lost any weight but boy can she climb a tree." *(They are convulsed.)*

GRAVEDIGGER. There are no more the likes of Henny Yorick around.

HAMLET. Yes, comedy has fallen on hard times.

GRAVEDIGGER. You can say that again.

HAMLET. Yes, comedy has fallen on hard times *(The two laugh again.)*

(A funeral procession approaches. We hear moaning and sobbing.)

HAMLET. Hark! A funeral approaches and we're not dressed for it. Let's hide in the bushes and discover who passed over this mortal veil.

GRAVEDIGGER. Right.

HAMLET. You're my kind of guy.

(They go off just as a weeping and moaning LAERTES enters followed by CLAUDIUS, GERTRUDE and BERNARDO who drag the coffin on.)

LAERTES. Why? Why did she do it? Why did she do it, my sweet, sweet sister.

HAMLET. *(Runs out to audience.)* Ophelia? Oh, no. It is Ophelia they're burying. *(Runs off.)*

CLAUDIUS. Why she decided on such a desperate course, I'll know not never why.

HAMLET. *(Runs back out to audience.)* She took her own life. she killed herself. *(Runs off.)*

GERTRUDE. Fare thee well, Ophelia. I had hoped that

one day thou wouldst be Hamlet's wife, but I guess it wasn't in the cards, kiddo.

CLAUDIUS. What grief, what grief. That's why I like stag parties better. *(BERNARDO pushes the coffin forward. LAERTES throws himself on top of it.)*

LAERTES. No, no, don't. Bury me instead. Please bury me instead. Throw the dirt on my face.

GERTRUDE. What bravado. What a beau geste!

(HAMLET comes from behind the bushes.)

HAMLET. Nay! Fiddlesticks! Forty thousand brothers could not with all their quantity of love make up my sum. *(HAMLET yanks away LAERTES and throws himself on the coffin.)* Bury me instead!

LAERTES. Hey! I was here first.

GERTRUDE. It's Hamlet!

CLAUDIUS. And still a pain in the ass.

HAMLET. Ophelia! Ophelia! No more to Ophelia!

LAERTES. Go away! Get your own dead sister. *(LAERTES starts to pull HAMLET away from the coffin. As he does, the lid comes off.)*

HAMLET. Oh, no. Look what you did. *(All but HAMLET back away.)* Oh, my beautiful passed away Ophelia, forgive us. Forgive us. *(He looks into the coffin. It's empty.)* She's not in it! Ophelia's not in the coffin!

GERTRUDE. Of course not. Ophelia's in Athens. In her depression she ran off with a Greek musician.

CLAUDIUS. It was awful. He had the only trombone in Denmark.

GERTRUDE. Do you know what it's like eating grape

leaves without music?

LAERTES. She's dead to us now. This funeral makes it final, and frankly I think we did it in good taste, don't you?

HAMLET. *(Looks at them all for a beat and runs off, saying.)* Mad, mad. The world's gone mad.

GERTRUDE. Poor Hamlet. Still as confused as ever.

LAERTES. What do we do now, my Lord?

CLAUDIUS. Now? Now? Now we prepare to bury a real dead person.

LAERTES. *(Puts his arm around the King.)* You're so mean. I like you.

BLACKOUT

Scene 9

Throne Room. HAMLET strumming a banjo.

HAMLET. *(Singing sadly.)*
OPHELIA, OPHELIA, I MISS YOU OOH, OOH, OOH.
OPHELIA, OPHELIA, YEAH, I DO, OOOOOH.
I'M SAD, NOT GLAD, CAUSE OH, I'VE GOT IT BAD.
OVER YOU, OOH, OOH, OOH.

GHOST. *(enters)* I'm not sure who I want killed more.

Your uncle or your music teacher.

HAMLET. I'm in torment, Father. Do you have any idea what it's like to have loved and lost?

GHOST. If I did, I'd be alive today.

(HORATIO enters.)

HORATIO. Hamlet, I come with a message from King Claudius. He wants you and Laertes to make up.

HAMLET. Done!

HORATIO. And to prove that there is no more bad blood between you, he has arranged a friendly duel.

HAMLET. A duel to show our friendship? Couldn't we just go out together and have a couple of beers?

HORATIO. It's what the King has asked for.

GHOST. A duel? Of course. A friendly duel might just be the answer. I'll remove the guard on your sword and right then and there you'll kill good ole Claude.

HAMLET. There'll be no more murder.

GHOST. Oh, come on. What's one more?

HAMLET. I've learned my lesson. I'm through seeking revenge. From now on I'm going to lead a pure, wholesome, contented and uncomplicated life.

GHOST. You know you're killing your father, don't you?

HAMLET. I don't care. It's a new Hamlet you're talking to. Screw revenge. To me the most important thing in my life is going to be love and peace and kindness and goodliness and singing. *(He sings.)*
WOE WOE WOE WOE
I MISS OPHELIA SO

MY HEART'S A SAD SAD MESS
AND THAT IS NO B. S.
(HAMLET exits. The GHOST follows him.)
GHOST. Hey, what if you just sang to Claudius for a couple of hours? Maybe that would kill him.

(GHOST exits just as CLAUDIUS and LAERTES enter and cross the stage.)

CLAUDIUS. Yes, a friendly duel is the answer. Except that the tip of your sword shall have no guard on it.
LAERTES. I like that.
CLAUDIUS. And it shall be dipped in poison.
LAERTES. I like that.
CLAUDIUS. And I'll also poison his wine.
LAERTES. I like that, too.
CLAUDIUS. I'll sprinkle poison on his toilet seat and even poison the toilet paper.
LAERTES. And if that doesn't work, I'll kill him.

(They exit as GERTRUDE and ROSENCRANTZ enter.)

GERTRUDE. Until I met you, Rosencrantz, I was only half a Queen.
ROSENCRANTZ. Does that beat two tens?
GERTRUDE. I know now my marriage to Claudius was a serious mistake. He's dull, he doesn't take me anywhere, he doesn't buy me anything, he's not that good-looking, and worse than that I find him very superficial.
ROSENCRANTZ. You know what I think? I think we ought to get rid of him.

(ROSENCRANTZ exits right, just as GUILDENSTERN enters right. He walks with GERTRUDE who continues the conversation.)

GERTRUDE. Get rid of the King? Of course. There's no alternative.
GUILDENSTERN. Let me get this straight. You want me to get rid of the King?
GERTRUDE. What a wonderful idea. I'm glad you thought of it.
GUILDENSTERN. Yes. And what's even better, I have the perfect solution.
GERTRUDE. I knew I picked the right man.
GUILDENSTERN. Don't worry, Queen. I'll come up with something so shocking, so diabolical, so scheming ... you'll think I'm part of the family. *(GUILDENSTERN exits left. GERTRUDE turns to the audience.)*
GERTRUDE. Actually, I'm not a bad woman. I'm really thinking of Claudius. If I sue him for divorce, it becomes a mess. There's the scandal, the accusations, the innuendos. He screams, I scream. No, murdering a husband is the only solution. At least this way we remain friends.

(She exits. HORATIO and HAMLET enter.)

HORATIO. Please, my Lord, I beg you not to enter this foolish contest. Laertes is the finest swordsman in all Europe. You, on the other hand, are a reknowned clumsy oaf.
HAMLET. That's the difference between you and the new me, Horatio. I refuse to look on the negative side of

things from now on.

HORATIO. I'm not negative, my Lord. I just know nothing ever works out for the best.

HAMLET. Poor, poor Horatio. How sad it is for a person so young to be a realist.

(BERNARDO enters.)

BERNARDO. All hail the King!

(CLAUDIUS, GERTRUDE and LAERTES enter.)

HAMLET. My Lord. My Lady. *(He kneels.)*
GERTRUDE. My son, the Prince. *(CLAUDIUS and GERTRUDE sit.)*
CLAUDIUS. *(Aside to Laertes.)* Try not to get him in the chest. He's wearing my shirt.
HAMLET. *(Pinching BERNARDO'S cheek.)* Hi, Bernie. Beautiful day, huh?
BERNARDO. No. It's raining.
HAMLET. Well, it's beautiful to me. Ah, my good Mother, good Stepfather, I have good news. I've reformed. I've changed my ways. No longer am I going to be mad at anyone. I'm going to be forgiving, and understanding, and tolerant. No longer will thy son believe in ghosts and spirits or be influenced by royal hallucinations.
CLAUDIUS. *(Not interested.)* Fine. Fine.
HAMLET. From now on, I'm going to be a model law abiding citizen, never crossing in the middle of the road but always at the corner, never spitting at peasants or

giving ye olde finger to the priests. From now on I'm going to do nothing but enjoy the peace and serenity that has made Denmark the great innocuous nation that it is.

CLAUDIUS. *(Offering a cup to HAMLET.)* Good, good. Now how about a cup of wine before the big fight, Hamlet?

HAMLET. No, thank you. Wine only makes me crave a woman of the night and I have sworn to become a goody-two-shoes.

CLAUDIUS. *(Producing a roll of toilet paper.)* Then how about some toilet paper for your nose?

HAMLET. I don't need anything. From now on, I'm going to look at the brighter side of things. I'm going to have a sense of humor, laugh, be gay. No more melancholy moods for this little pussycat.

CLAUDIUS. Fine. Now, let's get on with the match.

HAMLET. Life is for the living and that's the way it's always going to be in this Prince's mind. Revenge is a negative action and, as far as I'm concerned, all those still enamored with the idea can take it and shove it. Furthermore ...

GERTRUDE. Okay, Hamlet, That's it. You're giving us a headache.

CLAUDIUS. Okay, now oñst with this duel. I want everything to be fair and square. Here's for you, Laertes. *(He hands LAERTES his sword.)*

LAERTES. Thank you, my Lord.

CLAUDIUS. And this is for you, Hamlet. *(He hands HAMLET a much shorter sword.)*

HAMLET. *(Looks at sword and then at audience.)* That's

okay. I don't mind, for I have learned to be happy with my lot. Is it not the wise man who is the fool to be discontent with what he doesn't know, or is it the fool who is the wise man to be content with what he does know? I don't know. All I know is the moon belongs to everyone, the best things in life are free.

(The GHOST enters.)

GHOST. Okay, Hamlet, you got the sword, now get the King.
HAMLET. Stand out of the way, you miserable Ghost.
LAERTES. Pray, who he-eth talketh to?
GHOST. I'm not going anywhere until you get rid of that rotten brother of mine. Onest and for all.
HAMLET. Nay, I won't.
GHOST. Yay, you will.
HAMLET. Nay, I can't.
GHOST. Yay, you must.
CLAUDIUS. Who's he talking to?
BERNARDO. Once a wacko, always a wacko.
GHOST. For the last time, Hamlet, get rid of Claudius.
HAMLET. Better I get rid of you, dear father. *(HAMLET lunges at the GHOST. His sword passes through him, under his arm, and stabs BERNARDO.)*
BERNARDO. Thanks a lot. *(He falls.)*
GHOST. Ha, ha! You missed.
HAMLET. Well, I won't miss this time. *(HAMLET then pursues the GHOST.)*
CLAUDIUS. Gertrude, what is your rotten kid up to now?

GERTRUDE. I am puzzled, too, my Lord. Maybe the three of us should go to a family counselor.

GHOST. You must avenge me.

HAMLET. Never. If you didn't mix in, I'd have Ophelia and a hit show still running.

CLAUDIUS. *(to LAERTES)* You'd better get him before he wipes out the whole castle.

LAERTES. Right. *(He leaps to HAMLET.)* Okay, Hamlet, en garde.

HAMLET. Later.

HORATIO. Listen, Hamlet, as your friend as well as your pal, I'd like to say ... *(Still jabbing at the GHOST, HAMLET runs HORATIO through.)* ... Goodbye, Betty.

HAMLET. Now look what you made me do.

GHOST. You know you're not going to have many friends left. *(LAERTES jumps in front of HAMLET once more.)*

LAERTES. Will you stop flitting and fight. En garde!

HAMLET. Not now! *(HAMLET runs off after the GHOST.)*

GERTRUDE. All this excitement gives me a thirst. *(She picks up the goblet of wine intended for HAMLET and drinks it.)*

CLAUDIUS. *(alarmed)* Don't drink that wine.

GERTRUDE. Why not?

CLAUDIUS. I can't say, but do you know any single girls in town.

(ROSENCRANTZ and GUILDENSTERN enter.)

ROSENCRANTZ. *(Eating an apple.)* The King is as good as dead.

GUILDENSTERN. *(Eating a hero sandwich.)* You're telling me. I poisoned the apples.

ROSENCRANTZ. You didn't have to. I poisoned the hero sandwiches. *(They look at what they're eating and react in terror.)*

ROSENCRANTZ & GUILDENSTERN. Schmucks! *(They stagger and drop. HAMLET is now pursuing the GHOST and being pursued by LAERTES.)*

LAERTES. Fight me, Hamlet! Fight me!

HAMLET. Later.

LAERTES. Now!

GERTRUDE. *(Clutching her throat.)* Hamlet! Hamlet!

HAMLET. What? *(HAMLET stops, turns toward his mother and accidently stabs LAERTES.)*

LAERTES. Ahhhh! I think I'm going to have to say goodnight sweet Prince. *(He falls dead.)*

HAMLET. Sorry.

GERTRUDE. Hamlet! Hamlet!

HAMLET. *(Running to his mother.)* Mother!

GERTRUDE. I'm dying. The wine was poisoned.

HAMLET. Are you sure, Mother? Maybe it was just a bad year.

GERTRUDE. No. I know good wine, I know crappy wine and I know poisoned wine.

HAMLET. Maybe it was Norwegian wine.

GERTRUDE. I am finished. Have fun, son, because life is short. *(She dies on her throne.)*

CLAUDIUS. *(Rising and backing off in fear.)* I can explain. You see, I didn't know she was going to drink the wine. *(He hides behind the GHOST.)*

HAMLET. It's not your fault, Uncle Claudius. It's his

fault. *(indicating the GHOST)* If I wasn't so busy with this ghost, I would have drunk it and not Mother.

GHOST. I get blamed for everything.

HAMLET. *(Lunges at the GHOST.)* Take this! *(HAMLET'S sword gets CLAUDIUS.)*

CLAUDIUS. Oh, boy. This is gonna take a while to heal.

HAMLET. Alas, alas. I've slain the King.

CLAUDIUS. Hamlet, forgive me for everything. I know I was a cad, a crook, a liar, a cheat ... but mark my word, one day in the future those will be considered leadership qualities. *(He dies.)*

GHOST. I'm avenged. Good going, kid.

HAMLET. Oh, no. I've killed everyone in the castle. What am I gonna do when I need my sheets changed?

(OPHELIA enters with a suitcase. She is very pregnant.)

OPHELIA. Hamlet.

HAMLET. Ophelia.

OPHELIA. Oh, Hamlet, you're not dead in England.

HAMLET. No, but you're still knocked up in Denmark. *(He opens his arms to her. He still has his sword.)* My Ophelia! My Ophelia! *(He goes to her.)*

OPHELIA. *(She waddles toward him.)* My Prince. My Prince. *(As HAMLET gets closer to OPHELIA he realizes he has his sword and lays it on the ground. They embrace and kiss.)*

HAMLET. My dearest, sweetest Ophelia. What happened to the Greek musician?

OPHELIA. Very sad. The day before we were to be married, he ran off with the Duke of Chablis. Oh,

Hamlet, misfortune seems to be my strong suit.

HAMLET. Not any more, Ophelia. Now that we're together, I'll never let you go.

OPHELIA. You mean it?

HAMLET. May my mother drop dead if I'm lying.*(GERTRUDE lets out a moan and falls from the throne.)*

OPHELIA. Oh, Hamlet, you've finally become an adult. I'm so glad. In your childish state this could very well have become a tragedy, you know.

GHOST. *(approaches)* Excuse me, Son. I've come to say goodbye.

HAMLET. Father. Look, Ophelia, it's my father. He's smiling. He's happy. I'll bet now's a good time to ask him for a new pair of tights.

OPHELIA. You're still a flake, but I love you.

GHOST. I'm leaving now. I'm avenged. Thank you, Son. Farewell, sweet Prince.

HAMLET. Are you going to Heaven now, Father?

GHOST. *(Backing off and fading away.)* Yes... yes, I can see it now, son. Yes, it's Heaven.

HAMLET. Pray tell before you go, Father, what's it like?

GHOST. It has Golden Arches and they serve hamburgers.

OPHELIA. *(She and Hamlet are all alone.)* Hamlet.

HAMLET. Ophelia. At last. Together like we should be. Like we were meant to be.

OPHELIA. Yes, so what now, my Lord?

HAMLET. Now we will go on, you and I, and make a life for ourselves. And we will have a child. *(He looks at Ophelia's stomach.)* A big one. A boy, and we will call him

Michael Jackson. And he will sing and dance and make lots of money and maybe, just maybe, we can sell him this cold and silly country.

OPHELIA. The poor bastard.
HAMLET. And the rest is silence.

CURTAIN

SETS

The play can be done with a minimum of scenery. A curtain serving as the back drop and two easy-to-move stools or chair-high wood blocks are really all that is needed.

COSTUMES

The principals should all wear authentic costumes indigenous to their roles. However, Francisco could wear an army coat and a World War I metal helmet. Bernardo could wear a Beefeater hat and coat and Horatio could wear a leather motorcycle jacket. Rosencrantz and Guildenstern should both be dressed as Groucho Marx.

PROP LIST

ACT ONE

Scene 1
    Swords for Horatio & Francisco

Scene 2
    Staff for Bernardo
    Comb for Laertes
    Sword for Hamlet
    A rose

Scene 3
    Suitcase and some clothes
    Cigarette paper and some tobacco

Scene 4
    Cigar for ghost (optional)

Scene 5
    Two books or two magazines
    Cookie Monster hand puppet
    Cape for Hamlet

Scene 6
    Inhaler for Ophelia
    Letter

Scene 7
    Yo-yo
    Dust cloth
    Contracts and pen

Scene 8
    Pad and pencil — two of each

Scene 9
    Cigarette joint
    Play poster
    Two small heads on a stick

ACT TWO

Scene 1
    Souvenir and refreshment tray
    Four telegrams

Scene 3
    Cigarette and matches for Gertrude

Scene 4
    Shopping bag filled with
    Gift wrapped boxes

Scene 5
    Fake club
    Letter
    Three travel tickets

Scene 6
>Comb and scissors for Bernardo
>Marijuana-type stems for Ophelia
>Sword for Laertes

Scene 7
>Hand telescope
>Hand lantern

Scene 8
>Shovel for grave digger
>A bush or two (optional)
>Human skull
>A coffin with the top loose

Scene 9
>Banjo or small stringed instrument
>Wine goblet
>Roll of toilet paper
>Regular sword for Laertes
>Very short sword for Hamlet
>An apple
>A hero sandwich
>Suitcase for Ophelia

www.ingramcontent.com/pod-product-compliance
Lightning Source LLC
Chambersburg PA
CBHW051410290426
44108CB00015B/2226